Fourteen Years Behind the Wall: They Said Thank You

Diana Spinney

Fourteen Years Behind the Wall: They Said Thank You

Diana Spinney

C. Becker Books Emporia, KS

Fourteen Years Behind the Wall: They Said Thank You
Copyright © 2019 Diana Spinney

All rights reserved. No part of this publication may be reproduced, distributed, or transmitted in any form or by any means, without prior written permission of the copyright holder.

C. Becker Books
1114 Commercial St.
Emporia, Kansas 66801

Printed in the United States of America

Curtis Becker, Editor/Layout and Design/Cover Design
curtis@curtisbeckerbooks.com
curtisbeckerbooks.com

Cover Photo: *The Burlington Record*

ISBN: 978-0-578-6110-6

Prologue	1
Chapter 1 And So It Began	5
Chapter 2 The Prison System	7
Chapter 3 The Beginning	9
Chapter 4 The Prison Before Inmates	11
Chapter 5 And Now We Have Students	15
Chapter 6 Uniforms	17
Chapter 7 The School Day Schedule	19
Chapter 8 The Education Setup	21
Chapter 9 I'm the New GED Teacher	23
Chapter 10 The GED Test: Part One	25
Chapter 11 The GED Test: Part Two	27

Chapter 12   29
Essays

Chapter 13   33
Lock Downs

Chapter 14   35
Audits

Chapter 15   37
Security

Chapter 16   39
Safety and Assults

Chapter 17   41
Segregation

Chapter 18   43
Sentencing

Chapter 19   47
7 Principals in My 14 Years

Chapter 20   49
Tutors

Chapter 21   53
The KCCC Library

Chapter 22   55
My Classroom

Chapter 23   59
Flowers

Chapter 24 PSNs	61
Chapter 25 Gifts	63
Chapter 26 Holidays	67
Chapter 27 Race and Age	69
Chapter 28 Names	71
Chapter 29 Graduations	73
Chapter 30 Classes I Taught for MCC	79
Chapter 31 Thank You	83
Chapter 32 Appreciation	95
Acknowledgements	103

Two roads diverged in a wood, and I,
I took the one less traveled by, and
that has made all the difference.

Robert Frost

Prologue

Things do not change; we change.

Henry David Thoreau

I was a teacher who was never going to teach again. That seeems a strange sentence to begin my story about teaching in a prison, but it is, or was, a promise I made to myself and actually kept for almost 30 years. I lived most of my life in Fort Collins, Colorado, graduated from FCHS and Colorado State University, married my high school sweetheart, and worked as assistant registrar at CSU for 8 years.

Then a job opportunity opened up for my husband which would necessitate moving to Kansas. I decided I could put to use my college degree: English with teacher certification. We selected our community based on who needed an English teacher, and so I was to be a junior high English teacher in Oakley, Kansas.

I was 30 years old and a little frightened about the changes that lie ahead but, as we crossed the state line in our big move to Kansas, there was a double rainbow over the highway just ahead, and it told me "You can do it!"

I loved the smallness of Oakley, Kansas–after Fort Collins, Colorado; the friendly store clerks, the smiling postmaster, the Halloween children's costume parade, the beautifully decorated Christmas trees in the middle of the Main Street intersections, the grocery store that would order anything you requested.

Our daughter was due to start second grade and we were offered a choice: the teacher in town who murdered the King's English or be picked up by bus and taken to the school in Monument where the 2nd grade teacher was known to throw erasers. Another beauty of a small town: choices. I picked the erasers, but our daughter said the teacher never threw erasers at her class.

They never tell you in your Education classes that you will need to sponsor extra-curricular activities. I was offered a choice of coaching Girl's Volleyball or becoming Pep Club Sponsor. Never having excelled in sports, I selected the Pep Club which involved making sloppy joes or carameled apples in my kitchen and transporting them to games played in Monument (7 miles from Oakley) to raise money for Pep Club.

Now to teaching. I had six classes with 30 in a class. When I saw that, my great plan to have at least one essay written per student every week went out the window.

Then came the news that we punched a time clock—a first for me! I thought teachers were salaried and therefore not subject to accounting for every minute in the school building. We were also told that we could not leave during the day and must eat lunch in the school cafeteria with the students. (Wonderful food; I gained 20 lbs. before Thanksgiving!)

I never saw a paycheck. Since we couldn't leave during the day, someone at school would deposit for us.

Then came the reality of 30 in a classroom. Such noise, and I couldn't quiet them. I would send one of the worst out in the hall to help the noise level, and the principal would ask me what was the matter with me that I had to put someone in the hall!

Lesson plans had to be submitted to the principal weekly, and I guess I had never felt so regulated. I had three students who never did anything: no daily work; therefore, no passing any quizzes or tests which yields an absolute 0 in the grade book. The teacher's meeting before grade time revealed that "You can't give F's."

My response was, "I don't give any grade; they have to earn it." I was in hot water again.

So, by the middle of May, I was done with teaching. But, that summer my daughter and I lived with my parents in Fort Collins while I finished work on my Master's Degree.

My parents (both retired teachers) said, "You can't quit!"

So, I, being the obedient daughter I always tried to be, said, "okay. One more year and that is it."

And it was. The school year was 1971-1972. Nixon had a freeze on all salaries, so I didn't even get the small amount that having a Master's Degree added to your salary.

My second daughter was born on November 29, 1972 in

Diana Spinney

Oakley, Kansas.
 And, I was never going to teach again!

1

And So It Began

*You are never too old to set another goal
or dream another dream.*

C.S. Lewis

In the spring of 1998, I was working with mentally disabled individuals who were capable enough to work in some jobs in our community and were brought down from the facility where they lived to our building on Main Street in Goodland, Kansas. This building was appropriately called The ABLE Center.

I received a call from the Chamber of Commerce office that there were individuals there wanting to know about what facilities were available in Goodland for mentally disabled children. These people were from Corrections Corporation of America, the company that was building a prison in Burlington, Colorado (30 miles from Goodland). They needed to know what was available, if needed, for children of future employees coming to work at the prison.

They had a list of all categories of people to be hired to work at the prison and, as I scanned the list, I saw Academic Instructor and Vocational Instructor. I was told that all inmates had to go to school if they did not have a GED or high school diploma.

I can't say where my mind was at the moment, but in the next few days, I began to think how interesting and different teaching in a prison could be.

I have to write here that I was the only person thinking this would be a good thing. My family was absolutely opposed, citing dangers that I hadn't thought about, but I questioned how they could know about.

My favorite story on this subject is that while attending a FCHS class reunion, my best friend said, "You can not work in a prison." and took me over to another male classmate and said, "Tell Diana that she can't work in a prison."

I don't remember exactly what he said, but I remember the expression on his face when he revealed that he was a warden in a Colorado prison!

So I applied for an academic instructor position at the Kit Carson Correctional Center after making sure that I would not have to wear a uniform or carry a gun. (My two requirements!)

My first day of employment was to be October 19, 1998 contingent on the following items:
- Successfully passing a background investigation
- Successfully passing a company-paid drug screening

2

The Prison System

Another of our unmet challenges is that there are more than 2.2 million Americans now in prison—most of the for nonviolent crimes. This is the highest incarceration in the world.

Jimmy Carter

CCA, Corrections Corporation of America, is a private prison system. The facility in Burlington, Colorado, was built to fill a need for housing inmates when the state facilities were full.

I believe, when the prison opened, there were 14 state prisons in operation. They needed the private prisons to hold the overflow.

I, being from Kansas, always wondered about our 3 state prisons being sufficient to hold our inmates.

KCCC, built in 1998, increased its size by at least one-third-six or seven years later because our numbers continued to grow. We started with 900 inmates and reached 1400 inmates with the new addition.

I was never quite sure about the sentencing times or reasons. I had some students that I wondered if I had the full understanding of what they were in for because of, in their words, too many drunk driving violations or breaking parole.

That is where I learned the phrase "killing my sentence" which means serve out my entire sentence and not be paroled which can be broken. This from a student returned to my class after I thought he was released on parole and on his way to better things.

I do have to say that I questioned why some of my students landed in prison, but I had to tell myself that I was not a Case Manager and did not know all the details in any case. The phrase "Mine is not to question why…" reverberated in my mind frequently. We do incarcerate in high numbers.

3

The Beginning

The beginning is the most important of the work.

Plato

My first week at Kit Carson Correctional Facility consisted of 40 hours of training. Some of what was said seemed designed to scare us off, but I chose to see it as being filled in on the worst that could ever happen.

One example I remember vividly was being told on the first day what to do if, as females, we were taken in a hostage situation.

"Pee on yourself."

I chose to think of this as a scare tactic. Our class numbered

Diana Spinney

39, but one did not return the second day. Unfortunately, she was to be our education secretary,

I learned that the Education Department would be made up of 4 academic instructors, a computer teacher, a life skills teacher, a librarian, 2 vocational instructors, a secretary and a principal.

I was looking at the fact that the horticulture teacher was still needed and took it as a sign that my husband, with a degree in horticulture, should give it a try. Unfortunately, he didn't think that way!

But I thought that this was going to be a very interesting job with something new to learn every day.

And there were two more weeks of training before the actual work begins.

4

The Prison Before Inmates

A foolish consistency is the hobgoblin of little minds.

Ralph Waldo Emerson

So, training is over and we have been shown our classrooms, but where are our students? No one seems to know when the first inmates will arrive, but in the meantime we are told that there are many and varied jobs we have for you to do.

Now, I am a person who finds pleasure in consistency, but I am trying to recall some of the many and varied jobs we did while waiting for inmates.

In our department one day, we cut up terrycloth washcloths and wrapped them with tape around the bottom of the chair legs in our classrooms. Sound proofing?

Another day, everyone was sent to the cells and positioned by a toilet with orders to flush on signal. Never figured that one out–but it was a newly built prison and I guess that was to check out the plumbing.

My favorite job was being sent to the library to open hundreds of cartons of books sent to fill the library shelves. Each book needed to be stamped every 100 pages with "Property of Kit Carson Correctional Center." I didn't see how books could be stolen from a prison library, but I love books and it was wonderful to see the great selection of books that would stock the KCCC library shelves

During this waiting time we were assigned what class we would teach. In the academic area there was Adult Basic Education 1,2,3, and 4. All inmates would have to go to school if they did not already possess a high school diploma or GED. Inmates were tested as to what level they would be assigned. ABE 1 was for inmates testing at the 1st and 2nd grade level, ABE 2 for approximately 3,4,5,and 6th grade level. ABE 3 for 7th and 8th grade, and then ABE 4 for testing at above the 8th grade level.

I was assigned ABE 1 and protested. I was a secondary level teacher but was told that coming from working with mentally challenged individuals that I would have more of the patience that is needed with ABE 1 students.

My principal had evidently seen the roster of the first inmates who were coming to KCCC and asked if I had a Vietnamese dictionary at home because one of my students was Vietnamese and did not speak English. Did that ever raise my anxiety level!

But, the days dragged on and I believe it was at least three weeks before we got the word that the inmates were on their way.

Fourteen Years Behind the Wall: They Said Thank You

We were told to report back to the prison at 7 or 8 o'clock on a cold wintry night to help check in our first inmates. Well, it was closer to midnight before they arrived, and it was hard for me to be upbeat as I saw my first inmates in chains ambling in to the check stations. It was—in my eyes—a pretty sorry sight!

5

And Now We Have Students

There are far better things ahead than any we leave behind!

C.S. Lewis

What can I say about my first day of class? I have some memories that will live with me forever.

First, my initial anxiety was put to rest when I met my Vietnamese student whose name I can't remember, but it sounded like High Wind to me, so that is how I pronounced it. And, secondly, he came accompanied by a Vietnamese tutor whose English was wonderful. Together we made a great team to help High Wind learn to read in English.

I must insert here that my big problem in being assigned

Diana Spinney

ABE 1 is that I am a secondary teacher and never had any training in teaching reading to anyone. But, with my Vietnamese tutor, we formed a great team, and what a thrill it was the day that High Wind said, "I can read, I can read!"

The 8 remaining students in my ABE 1 class were Spanish and I spoke no Spanish, but their English was OK. After passing out the beginner workbooks, I bent over to help an older mustached student. I looked at his arm and hand before me and they were solidly tattooed clear out to his fingernails. I stood up and heard, very clearly, my mother's voice–she's long deceased–saying, *Diana, what are you doing in this place?* A little giggle rose up in my throat and soon became uncontrollable as I headed to step outside the classroom door to get control of myself.

And that was my first day of teaching ABE1 at Kit Carson Correctional Center.

6

Uniforms

Another place where you can always tell a man by his clothes is prison.

Anonymous

When I considered applying to work in the prison, I had two items that I could not do. I did not want to wear a uniform and I would not carry a gun. Fortunately, I found out that neither of those would apply. No one carried a gun in the prison (they were all locked up) and secondly, officers wore uniforms, teachers did not.

I guess I was surprised—or maybe startled is the word—to see my first class wearing bright orange. I immediately thought of the two orange items in my closet and vowed never to wear them again.

Piper Kerman, who wrote the best-selling book and now television series *Orange Is the New Black*, is quoted as saying after her term in prison, "I do like the color orange. Before I went to prison, I would wear it. I think it's an energetic, creative color. I do not wear it any longer." (That goes for me, too!)

And, perhaps, the prison officials decided it was too energetic for the inmates to wear, because, for whatever the reason, in a short time, inmates were issued dark green uniforms. The orange uniforms were used for inmates in segregation.

But, while I am on the topic of inmate dress, I should go into teacher dress. We did not have to wear a uniform as the security officers did, but there were a few requirements. I think the rules of no open-toed shoes, no sleeveless tops, and no dangling earrings were for our own safety and were not hard to follow. I didn't understand the no denim rule.

A postscript on the dark green uniforms: Several years after the dark green uniforms were put into use, I had cataract surgery on both eyes and was told that I would now see colors as much brighter and more clear. I now saw inmates in varying shades of green yielding mostly two-tone uniforms. The constant washing had not been good to the dark green color!

7

The School Day Schedule

*God grant me the Serenity to accept the things I cannot change,
Courage to change the things I can,
and Wisdom to know the difference.*

Reinhold Niebuhr

All teachers had 2 classes a day. We were to be in our classrooms from 7 to 10 A.M. for morning class and 1 to 4 P.M. for afternoon classes. Each session had different students. We took attendance on 'out count sheets' that were picked up after each session started. If an inmate was not in his cell, he had to be somewhere else or accounted for–in segregation, in medical, or in class.

Our class time would be cancelled at a time of a company audit, a lockdown, or a special activity which I'll go into in further detail in future chapters.

A couple occasions of no class remain in my mind that occurred because of outside events.

My diary page on May 23: "I'd best not let this day pass without comment. This was the inmate barbecue and game day, so classes were cancelled and teachers were to report for outside duty. I spent the afternoon in outside rec, and I know in my time here, I have never seen so many inmates in one place–maybe 400? I kept thinking that it only takes one. But everyone was on their best behavior enjoying volleyball, softball, horse shoes, foot races, tug-of-war plus watermelon and ice cream cones. They didn't even dump their trash anywhere but in trash cans. An amazing day!"

My diary page on August 18: "Now I know what only a little tear gas can do to you. It wafted out from segregation to the gazebo outside where we were eating our lunch and was very irritating. I suppose it was much more to all the inhabitants of segregation. Our students had been sent home at 10:10, not to return all day."

There was no school when lockdowns occurred because teachers were either assigned to help search cells or help in the kitchen (in place of the inmate cooks).

The biggest problem for me when audits or lockdowns occurred was in scheduling GED testing because we did not have advance notice of these events.

8

The Education Setup

Education is the period during which you are being instructed by somebody you do not know, about something you do not want to know.

Chesterson

At this point, you might be wondering how we keep our classes filled-what with inmates transferring into the prison and, likewise, transferring out to another facility. Plus, at the GED level, they complete their GED and graduate.

When an inmate entered our prison, and he did not have a GED or high school diploma, he was given a test that determined what level of instruction he was ready for. The test was called the TABE Test or the Test of Adult Basic Education.

If he tested below the 3rd grade level, he was placed in an

Diana Spinney

ABE I class, 3rd and 4th grade level was ABE II, and 5th and 6th grade level was ABE III or preGED. If he tested at the 7th grade level or above, he was placed in the GED class.

The students in ABE I, II. and III were given the TABE Test every 3 months, and this test would determine if they had learned enough in this class to advance to the next level.

You can see that each teacher has a lot of comings and goings at whatever level he is teaching.

I have this quote from my diary dated September 3: "I am grateful for my new batch of students moved up from preGED. All but one are gung-ho to get their GED. It is fun to watch them work."

9

I'm the New GED Teacher

'Tis a gift to be simple,
'Tis a gift to be free'
'Tis a gift to come down
Where we ought to be
And when we find ourselves
In the place that's right
"Twill be in the valley
Of love and delight.

A Ninth Century Shaker Hymn

I know that I mentioned earlier that my assignment to ABE I did not make me happy, but I don't think a year had passed before the ABE IV (GED) instructor left the prison for other employment and I got moved to the GED classroom. I was thrilled!

But, even though I was where I thought I should be, that is, the GED class, and most days were filled with more ups than downs, it wasn't always sunshine and roses.

Here are some excerpts from duties that called me away from my class and/or caused cancellation of GED classes:

•April 3 - sent to teach a Report Writing Class to officers whose writeups were not always clear and/or legible.

•May 7 - CCA Audit - students remain in their cells.

•June 13 - survived another lockdown - sent to the picket to see their duties

•July 10 -teachers to help out in Rec due to shortage of officers.

•August 18 - tear gas caused a lockdown

But, my big responsibility, I thought, was to learn all I could, as quickly as I could, about the GED test. There was a lot to it; plus how and when I could schedule it, and what was the best way I could prepare my students to take and pass it?

10

The GED Test: Part One

You can steer yourself in any direction you choose.

Dr. Suess

In explaining the GED test to my students, I had to remember that they had not graduated from high school and were not used to taking tests and, in fact, the word TEST probably conjured up some terrible memories to some.

So, I told them that the GED test consists of 5 subjects: Reading, Science, Social Studies, Mathematics, and Writing Skills. The first three are based on your ability to read the question and select an answer from multiple choices.

The Math test contained a little Algebra and Geometry but

was multiple choice.(This was the subject failed most frequently, but there were three versions of each test so the inmate had three trys in one year to pass the Math test.

Writing Skills was my biggest concern because it was multiple choice questions and an essay question. More on this in Chapter 12.

To prepare for a test, we had large English study books, but no Spanish books. (The GED test was available to us in English, Spanish, and French–the latter obviously not needed.) But, I did have many students testing in Spanish. I found this entry in a diary that I kept early on.

> I am so upset over the plight of my Spanish students. I've hollered for three years about it and nobody listens. I do not speak Spanish, but I wasn't hired on the basis that I could. Now Mr. Trimmer, the best principal I ever had, says to buy whatever Spanish books I need. I already have. Every time I got to the bookstores, I bought their Spanish GED testing books–paid for them myself! (Now I'll get a few more - with prison money!)

I need to give you one more fact about the GED test. The GED test is rewritten every ten years. So I was in on one of those times. An inmate had to have passed all five tests in December before the new test came out or start over. That December was heavily scheduled!

11

The GED Test: Part Two

There are no such things as limits to growth because there are no limits on the human capacity for intelligence, imagination, and wonder.

Ronald Reagan

So, the inmate selects whatever GED test he wants to start with: Reading, Science, Social Studies, Mathematics, or Writing Skills. He takes the mockup test in the front of the study book and, if he misses ten questions or less, he is ready for the Official Practice Test. (If not, there is much to study in those big books to get ready,) The Official Practice Tests are kept in a locked cabinet to which I had the only key.

If he scores a passing grade on the OPT, his name goes on the board for the next testing time which occurs twice a month.

Diana Spinney

There are 3 versions of each official GED test each year so the student has 3 chances in a calendar year to pass a test–and I can tell you right now that the 3 times and out occurred most often in Math! One student finally passed Math after 6 tries–that's 2 years in class. I believe his mother–after a few phone calls to me urging me not to let him quit–talked another inmate outside of my class to help him and it worked! (See the chapter on Graduations for more on this California mother's assistance.)*

I have to express great appreciation at this time for our official GED tester. She worked as an employee of Morgan Community College and her name is Adrienne Fasse. I can't say how much she meant to the GED program, and how much she still means to me. Her availability as GED tester enabled KCCC to have a high number of GEDs each year,

I noted in the instructions I left for my successor as the new GED instructor that, although Adrienne Fasse has been our official GED tester since testing began at the facility, she is still considered a visitor and must be escorted in to our classroom and out to the front hall. She is also not to be left alone with inmates. That's a laugh because she had to be alone when testing inmates in my room because neither I nor a guard was allowed to be in the room during testing time! I did sit right outside the door.

*This is a good place to add that in my entire time as a prison teacher, I received only two phone calls from mothers of inmates: one noted above from California and the other from a mother whose son was sent to segregation. She wanted to know why!

12

Essays

Don't try to walk before you crawl.

Proverb

The essay part of the Writing Skills GED Test presented a challenge to me because, even though I have a bachelor's degree and a master's degree in English and had taught junior high English for two years, I had to help these grown men—who maybe had never written anything, possibly even a letter home—write a passable essay.

One student's practice essays were almost like reading a foreign language. I found out that he had dropped out of school after 4th grade and lived in an abandoned trailer since both parents were in prison. I found an elementary spelling book and we worked from there. I believe he passed he passed the Writing Skills GED Test on the third try. (You are allowed three tries a year!)

My favorite memory in essay writing involved an inmate, maybe 50 years old , who wrote a practice essay about hopping trains. I need to say here that I learned a lot from my student's practice essays, but hopping trains was a peak learning experience for me. (And it was well written, too!)

Now, I was not allowed to see any completed essay tests as Mrs. Fasse collected them and would take them immediately out of the prison to the college where they were sent out for scoring.

But, I asked if I could please see my "hopping trains" man's essay. I could then know his topic and go from there. His topic was a memorable experience in his life and he wrote about climbing Kilimanjaro at the age of 12 with the man who had taken him in from the foster care system in Chicago. It was well written, and I learned a lot in reading it.

From climbing Mt. Kilimanjaro to hopping trains to prison. Do you see why I loved my teaching in the prison? Ever a new day and a new learning experience, and I learned that at age 60+, you are never too old to learn.

The following are some examples from notes I received when an inmate was ill - to explain his absence. I wish I could just make copies, but this will have to do.

"I'm not filling good I'm trying to get this wright up droped but I will see you tomorrow for the test."

"I am real sick and I am thoughing up."

"I am still not fellingwell I will not miss no more days only sweatloged."

"I would like to notify Princeable Horton that I am feeling sick."

These are just a few of many notices I received, but offer some explanation of why I worried about an inmate passing the GED Writing Skills Test.

13

Lock Downs

Since we cannot change reality, let us change the eyes which see reality.

Nikos Kazantzakis

Lock downs were not my favorite times at the prison. I suppose they are essential to make sure that there is no contraband in the inmate's cell. But, as teachers with our students locked down, we were either assigned to search cells or work in the kitchen since the inmate kitchen workers were locked in their cells.

Inmates were only allowed three books and two rolls of toilet paper in their cells and that seemed to be the only items that we would find that were over the number allowed.

I didn't like the times when the cells I was searching belonged

Diana Spinney

to my GED students. Even though they were out on the floor when we searched, they could see who was searching their cell and it just bothered me.

I'm sure it was just the adjustment to our everyday schedule that was the most upsetting. I found this notation in my diary from June 7:

> Another 'scoop' has gone awry! I was told last Tuesday that June 10-11-12 would be a lockdown. Top Secret! But I was told so I could change the GED testing set for June 11. This morning inmates told me that we were going to have a lockdown - so much for secrecy and getting the jump on things!
>
> Inmates always knew more than we did!

14

Audits

To affect the quality of the day, that is the highest ot arts.

Henry David Thoreau

I think this is a good place to explain why I believed that audits were necessary. Kit Carson Correctional Facility was a private prison that was filled with inmates that the Colorado State prisons had run out of room for. So, CCA worked on a renewable contract with the state to stay in business.

The private prison had to provide each inmate they housed with the exact number of items they would have been provided with in the state system; that is, number of t-shirts, uniforms, etc., plus similar menus and amount of food served, and educational choices which included Life Skills and Computer Technology.

That explained the audits to me. CCA had to be sure we were doing everything according to the book.

From my diary dated May 7:

A CCA audit is over, the debriefing really told us nothing. The specifics were not given, but I had thought we would be OK. On the whole, people do their jobs to the best of their ability - I hope!

15

Security

As the world becomes more and more civilized, it puts more and more things under lock and key.

Unknown

I'm not sure where security fits into this memoir, but I do know that it has to be #1 in order for a prison to exist.

As employees, we were all required to take off our shoes and walk through through the electronic setup. This was no problem for me until I had a knee replacement. This set off the monitor and then I had to be wanded.

The two incidents I remember or was witness to involved cigarettes. The first year or so we were open, smoking was allowed. Then the state prisons, for health reasons, perhaps, banned smoking in their facilities, so KCC followed suit.

The first 'infraction' occurred when a tiny Asian female visitor on oxygen was searched only to discover a carton of cigarettes in the tank!

The second incident occurred right outside my classroom when I felt that there was too much attention being paid to the ceiling panels in the hallway. We climbed up on a chair and popped the ceiling panel to discover several packages of cigarettes stored there. I believe they were getting ready for the prison's soon-to-be no smoking policy.

Our main problem for several years was that the Education Department had no officer assigned to us. Ours was an area behind a locked door which consisted of five classrooms, the principal's office, a computer room, and a bathroom. We could not leave our room of students with no one to replace us, so it was a long wait to hit the bathroom!

The following is a quote from my diary dated July 10:

> I am maintaining my attitude of 'no fear' without an educational officer, but then when told that they worry about what might go on in our hallways, I say "Bring on an officer." because I can't even leave my room to go to the bathroom, let alone check on what the inmates are doing when they step out to the bathroom. But no officer available for Education.

I think it was about 2 years before we had an officer assigned to the Education Department.

16

Safety and Assults

*I am not afraid of storms,
for I am learning how to sail my ship.*

Louisa May Alcott

Just as I am learning to 'sail my own ship' in the classroom and doing so without any officer presence in the Education Department, two things happened that caused me some concern.

The first was a report of a teacher in the Limon State Prison who was the first into her department in the morning, and who was raped by an inmate apparently entering right behind her.

The second was a staff member killed in the kitchen by an inmate. This, too, occurred at the Limon facility.

We had a tour scheduled for our teachers to visit the Limon

prison, all or our ID's checked, etc., and it was cancelled. No more tours of the Limon prison allowed.

Shortly after this, I found an article giving number of assaults on prison staff in Arizona, published in *The Arizona Republic*. From the years 2005 to 2014, assaults on staff in state prisons increased from 149 to 412.

Assaults on staff in private prisons in the same years 2005 to 2014 went from 11 to 41.

So, after assimilating all of the above information, I decided to sail on. I had a heavy duty stapler in my top right-hand desk drawer and, if needed, I felt I could hit any attacker with it.

P.S. I think this chapter needs a P.S. I have been asked many times, "weren't you ever afraid in your classroom?" I'm not sure whether it was fear or anxiety, but I was on the two occasions when the prison lost its power. Actually, the entire city of Burlington lost its power at those times. I know that because when we headed out for lunch, no restaurant could serve because they had no power. We drove to Stratton for lunch!

But I say I had no fear at those two times because although we were in total darkness (there were no windows in our department in the middle of the prison), I just sat very still except for opening the drawer and putting my hand on my trusty stapler!

17

Segregation

Try to be a rainbow in someone's cloud.

Maya Angelou

Segregation was the name of the place where inmates were sent when they broke the rules. It was certainly not my favorite place to visit, but I would visit if I needed to get a study book to a student of mine who landed in there.

Mrs. Fasse and I gave the GED test to an inmate in segregation on at least two occasions when it would allow the inmate to complete his GED before being shipped out.

There were at least 20, maybe 30 cells, in the two-story segregation and often it was at capacity, so you can imagine the noise that occurred when two women, not in officer uniform, were allowed in.

Most reading I have done refers to what my prison called segregation as 'solitary confinement' and stated that it is to protect the facility and staff.

However, I felt that our prison sent inmates to segregation as more of a disciplinary measure because they broke the rules. Too many writeups and off to segregation.

I remember one day, my students were acting rather strangely and trying to get my attention, and I finally figured out that they were trying to tell me that I had left my cabinet keys hanging in the lock. They would be sent to segregation if they touched any keys so wanted me to get them in my pocket where they belonged.

And, of course, an inmate could not touch you or he would be sent to segregation. This never happened to me in the prison because, on the whole, they followed the rules in my classroom.

But, as I was reminded of this touching thing, it brought forth an incident that occurred on the first day I substituted at the local high school after retiring from the prison.

This was a 9th grade English class, and after I gave the assignment, I walked to the back of the class to keep an eye on things. This young man walked right up to me and hugged me. As he scanned the class for approval of his actions, I said, "If an inmate so much as touched me in my prison class, he would be sent to segregation." I didn't want to give him any more attention so the class went on studying and I sat down. But I will never forget it!

18

Sentencing

This chapter seems to me to require a sub-title of this question: Who should be sent to prison and why and for how long?

All I knew of Kit Carson Correctional Center when I applied was that it was a medium-security prison and, therefore, I assumed would not have any murderers housed there.

But, then there was my first Vietnamese student whose name I translated as "High Wind." My Vietnamese tutor and I got along famously with him and even taught him how to read in English.

He was anxious to get into an Anger Management class that was offered at KCCC, but it was a popular class and had a long waiting list. One day, he just blew up when finding out that they still didn't have room for him and shouted, "I must have Anger Management because I murdered someone." I'm sure happy that there were no cameras to record the look on my face when I heard that.

I did not know what my students were in prison for, but I

did learn an expression that involved sentencing when one of my students was paroled as he was just about to complete his GED. I was sad to lose him but happy that he was getting out of prison. But, a few months later, he was back and explained he'd had enough of keeping up with the parole rules and said, "I'm just going to kill my sentence." So he finished the full term of his sentence and earned his GED, too.

I do know that I had some students who were at KCCC with drug charges and, in one case, too many traffic violations. I couldn't understand this but, of course, I didn't have all the details because I wasn't their case manager.

I did wonder if we weren't sending some people to prison who, maybe, shouldn't be there—especially at a medium-security prison.

In 2015, I found an article in *NewsMax* magazine that seemed to go along with my thoughts. Former New York Police Commissioner Bernard P. Kerik was incarcerated and saw from the inside out that the cost of our criminal justice system was on the verge of imploding. He felt that the biggest flaw of our system is that we take regulatory, administrative violations and turn them into criminal conduct. (*NewsMax*, May 2015, page 45)

So, I think I saw a little of this with my limited knowledge of sentencing, but Mr. Kerik saw it as an economic catastrophe for our country. In 2015, we had some 2.3 million incarcerated in U.S. prisons. He felt we must have criminal-justice reform or our system will implode.

As I ponder this, I realize that maybe a little reform has taken place. CCA was a private prison system that came into the state of Colorado because their many state facilities were full and they didn't want to build more.

CCA worked under a contract from the state, and I believe it was reviewed yearly. Before I retired in 2013, we were already taking in inmates from Idaho and Wyoming to fill our beds.

Kit Carson Correctional Center closed down for lack of inmates in 2016.

Now I can ask myself: do we have less criminal activity going on in the state or Colorado, or is there some serious criminal justice reform going on?

19

7 Principals in My 14 Years

*A spelling tip: the principal is your pal.
(But I love princeable: one inmate's spelling)*

The setup for the Educational Department was like any school: a principal, and a secretary, but minus a superintendent.

My first principal was a short little man who wore bowties and reminded me of Woody Woodpecker. When he received the names of inmates headed our way, who would be in our classes, he asked if I spoke Vietnamese or had access to a Vietnamese dictionary. Since you can guess my answer, you will know how it helped me in the anxiety department as the first day of my prison teaching approached.

Diana Spinney

This principal wasn't with us too long before Mr. Fred Trimmer took over. He had recently retired from the 'regular school system,' but was certainly not ready to retire from education. I think of him still, today, as the Energizer Bunny: seemingly tireless, always ready to go, and truly supportive of his staff and our students. He wrote a column for the prison newspaper and was with us longer than any of my seven principals. And, he remains my favorite principal of all my teaching locations.

The five principals that followed kind of pass in a blur. I don't remember names and only remember one who scared some of us because we thought he suffered from PTSD.

20

Tutors

It wasn't until quite late in life that I discovered how easy it is to say "I don't know."

Somerset Maugham

It was very early on in my GED teaching when I had to say "I don't know." As I mentioned before, I do not speak Spanish and probably a third of my students were Spanish. They spoke English, but certainly wanted to take the Spanish version of the GED.

    I had two or three Spanish tutors over the course of 13 years who were excellent teachers. My biggest concern was the Spanish essay test because, since I didn't speak Spanish, I certainly could not help anyone write in Spanish. My Spanish tutors became experts in grading Spanish essays.

I had three English tutors over the years who were also wonderful. They had that special talent to get along with my GED inmates, which is a remarkable quality because inmates don't always want to 'take' something from fellow inmates—as in this case—instruction.

In the setup of the GED Math test, I also had to admit, mainly to my tutors, "I don't know." I had passed Algebra and Geometry with A's in high school, but I knew not to go beyond that point.

The GED test is rewritten every 10 years and seven years into my teaching the GED class, a new test was to come out. I need to insert here that you have to have all five tests passed before the new test begins, or you have to start over. You can imagine the scramble to have all five tests passed by December 31 of that test's final year. My tutors were calm amidst the scramble.

The hype on the new test also said that the Math test would include some Trigonometry.

I was as panic stricken as some of my students, but my tutors weren't and it didn't happen.

But, these excellent tutors helped to strengthen this English teacher's math skills, so that I, too, could have passed the GED Math test, even after graduating from high school 40 years ago.

I wish that I could name these remarkable tutors, but have decided it wouldn't be a proper thing to do, but their names and faces are forever etched in my memory bank. And I hope they are well and living happily out of prison.

P.S. You might be wondering how we obtained the tutors in our classrooms. We did not get to select them. All inmates had to have jobs in the prison and some had marked that they would like to work in the Education Department. So, they were assigned to us according to our needs and numbers. I was very lucky in the assigning because one of my tutors was a junior high teacher before coming to prison.

21

The KCCC Library

The only thing you absolutely have to know is the location of the library.

Albert Einstein

I know I mentioned earlier that one of our early assignments, before inmates arrived, was to open boxes of books for the library and stamp every 100 pages of each with the KCCC stamp.

I love books and libraries so this job was right up my alley. And, it was so much fun to see all of the great books sent to stock the shelves. Somebody made great selections.

There was also a section for law books which I am sure was a requirement of our contract with the state.* And, in addition, the library provided two typewriters for inmates to use in working on correspondence with their lawyers.

The library also subscribed to a significant number of magazines that were to be read in the library.

I also built up a small library in my classroom. I was buying books for myself and when finished would bring them to my classroom for students to check out.
Another prison rule: an inmate was allowed to have only three books in his cell at one time.

*These law books arrived every year, and by the end of my 14 years at KCCC, were taking up lots of room in the library. They added new shelving as often as they could, but the library had to remain its original size. It seemed smaller because it was somewhat overcrowded!

22

My Classroom

A room without books is like a body without a soul.

Cicero

One cabinet held your coat and personal items; another was a file cabinet for all my test results. They were locked cabinets and I had the keys for both plus my room door.

The mention of keys reminds me of an incident with my students one morning.

I think I need to write a little about my teaching room inside the prison.

First off, of course, there were no windows. There was one wall of white boards and a cork board on another wall. The rest of the walls were painted white cinderblock.

Assignments had been handed out, and I thought all would be calm and quiet for a while. But, I sensed an uneasiness in the room, some throat clearing and nodding directed toward me—and, finally, I noticed toward one of the cabinets I had left my keys hanging in the lock. I immediately retrieved them and found out later that if an inmate touched any keys he would be sent to segregation. But I felt they were trying to save me from getting a PSN because if a guard entered my room and saw those keys hanging, I would have been in trouble. (I always felt that my students would help me.) I was not afraid in the classroom.

Although, I might be fudging just a bit when I recall the several times that Burlington lost power. Can you visualize how dark a classroom within an entire department that has no windows can be? That's why I reached into my top desk drawer and grabbed my stapler. One shouldn't be totally weaponless in the total darkness!

There was a bookcase in the room to hold some of the GED study books, but I soon began to fill it with books that I bought and read and wanted to share. Many of my students loved it and always returned them. Some even added books that they had received from home. I soon requested another bookcase.

I loved decorating my bulletin board. My mother taught me when very young how to cut letters out of construction paper, so it was very easy to cut out letters of some of my favorite sayings and brighten up my room. I felt some were quite inspirational but one they openly argued about with me.

That was a Christmas posting of Virginia's letter to the editor of a newspaper asking if Santa Claus is real. His answer ended with BELIEVE. This led to some discussion on how I could possibly believe in Santa Claus. I loved their feedback, and it led to some great discussion.

The only bad thing I remember about my room was how cold it was. I mean I accumulated a lot of jacket outfits and even sometimes wore mittens. (I found it very hard to correct papers in mittens!) I do not know what happened, but after 7 or 8 years, it got warmer in my room, but I was still happy to have jacket ensembles!

23

Flowers

Earth laughs in flowers.

Ralph Waldo Emerson

Next to books, another item I enjoy looking at is a flower. I happen to be married to a man who graduated in horticulture, and he made sure that the outside of our home was surrounded by a great lawn, magnificent trees, and a variety of colorful flowers.

I suspected that many of my students had not grown up with this, and I figured I could at least bring flowers into my room for a little touch of beauty.

So, I shared roses, petunias, clematis, tulips, allium, pansies, and daffodils singly or in a small arrangement on my desk. I

Diana Spinney

soon learned that all they could identify was a rose.

I decided that floriculture was my addition to education outside of our GED books.

I love this quote from Hans Christian Anderson

> "Just living is not enough…one must have sunshine, freedom, and a little flower."

Since I couldn't deliver on the first two, I could at least offer a little flower.

24

PSNs

*To dry one's eyes and laugh at a fall,
and baffled, get up and begin again.*

Robert Browning

I think it is time in this memoir to confess that I didn't always do the right thing–or rather I made at least a couple of mistakes.

I had early on heard about PSNs but didn't know the details. I heard that if you received three PSNs, you were out of a job. So, I decided that PSN might mean 'pretty sad news'!

My first PSN was on my desk the morning after I had taught a college Speech class. The students were preparing to give speeches with visual props, so I brought in poster paper, glue, and my collapsible scissors to help them prepare.

Diana Spinney

From my diary:

I, unbelievably, left the scissors on my desk and they shook my room down over the weekend. I'm going to be grateful for having it pointed out to me that mentally I'm really slipping; need to sharpen up! I'm working on it.

My second PSN really surprised me! All the prison staff were gathered in the visitation room to hear the results of an audit. Pictures were passed around and there were many of GED graduations. I thought, since I had bought the film and paid for the developing that I would just take a couple for my scrapbook.

Two days later I was called in to the Assistant Warden's office so that he could deliver my second PSN. It was reported that I had taken two of the pictures being passed around and the Assistant Warden didn't want to hear any reason why I had stolen two pictures.

Did I spend my remaining years at the prison worrying about a third PSN? No, but there was something I continued to do that I knew the Assistant Warden was against, but that was not going to stop me.

You will understand why in the chapter titled "Gifts."

25

Gifts

And it is more blessed to give than to receive, so it must be more blessed to receive than to give back.

Robert Frost

If I haven't mentioned it before, it is time to make sure you know how much artistic talent resides within the prison walls.

When the prison opened, there was a shop room where inmates turned out some beautiful wood items which we could purchase. I have an octagon wood-framed CSU clock that I am looking at as I write this. I also gave Bronco clocks for Christmas gifts that first year. But, for some reason not given, the shop lasted only a couple of years and certainly shut down an outlet for many inmate's artistic talents.

Inmates could make beautiful things out of what little they had. Cutting, folding, and weaving potato chip wrappers into cars or whatever was a marvel to me. I received several cutout and standup cards which would be difficult for me to make. They knew I was a Bronco fan, and one cut and standup Bronco Stadium card complete with cheering crowd is among my Bronco treasures. They also made beautiful long-stem roses out of Kleenex or toilet paper. You had to see them to believe how beautiful and realistic they were.

I also have a collection of cards with their artwork on them. One specialty was sugar coating their artwork. The Spanish students, especially, used such bright colors in their cards and then sugarcoated them. I wish that I could share them with you, but don't know how to put them in this book.

> "Be sure you put your feet in the right place, then stand firm." -Abraham Lincoln

My chapter on PSNs reminded me that I had been warned not to accept any gifts from inmates. I found that impossible to do, and for one very good reason. I had been taught from a very young age that it is "more blessed to give than to receive." I felt very blessed when an inmate would give something he had made for me knowing that I could not give him anything in return except a 'thank you.' But, to reject a card or flower made for me was something I could not do.

My most vivid memory on this subject was when two of my students, in their forties at least, stood outside my door acting kind of funny. Both of them had just earned their GED, so no longer needed to come to class. (They would be in the next grad-

Fourteen Years Behind the Wall: They Said Thank You

uation as soon as we had at least 15 completing their GED). I wondered how they got out of their cells to come to the Education Department.

I opened the door and they handed me a beautiful personalized card, and there was no way I was going to refuse it. I guess I felt blessed that these men who were in prison and had to go to school could say 'thank you' for giving us the opportunity to achieve something while serving our time. (These two men each had a beautiful wife who attended their graduation and and came up to me during refreshment time and said, "Thank you.")

I did take any gifts from my students home immediately, as our rooms were subject to search at any time. And, I didn't need that third PSN!

26

Holidays

Do your little bit of good where you are, it's those little bits of good put together that overwhelms the world.

Archbishop Desmond Tutu

Holidays, any and all of them, are very important to me, and I wasn't sure how they were observed in a prison.

Inmates would have time off from school at holiday time because we were given the day off, but beyond that I didn't find much difference in their daily goings-on.

I believe it was the Salvation Army that gave bootie/sox to all inmates at Christmas and greeting cards for all occasions were always available to inmates who wanted them.

If family/visitors brought presents in at Christmas, they could not be wrapped because everything had to be inspected.

Thanksgiving and Christmas dinners were also special, and I think visitation went on for special holidays.

The Education Department had at least one big party for our tutors, and I had never seen such appreciation for the food put before them.

I believe in my later years at the prison, there were staff door decorating contests at Christmas, judged by the inmates.

But, I always found it a little difficult to bring the full spirit of any holiday into the prison.

27

Race and Age

Alberto Sanchez wrote to me:

Just wanted to thank you for helping me out in your classroom. Thank you for keeping in mind that regardless of our race differences, we are all God's children.

I was not sure how I was going to approach this subject in my memoir, but I'll just jump in to my initial observations and go from there.

My first class, ABE 1, was entirely Spanish except for 1 Black student and 1 Vietnamese. This was also the class that had my youngest ever student at age 17.

So, I decided to do some checking into the racial makeup of the prison and found that it averaged one-third Black, one-third Caucasion, and one-third Spanish with a few Indian and Orien-

Diana Spinney

tal thrown in.

In my younger students, the Spanish students had a much greater respect for me as their teacher than the young Blacks did.

My older students were all quite respectful and I had ages that ranged from 18 to 75.

I do not think I am particularly race conscious and do not like to describe anyone that way.

But, one day I was trying to describe a student who was black to my principal by talking about his bright eyes and infectious smile, but the principal finally asked me, "How black is he?"

I was too astonished to answer having never gotten into shades of black of the Negro race.

Enough said!

28

Names

Every man's first name is more important than his last, until he becomes famous.

Camus

I always addressed my students by last name preceded by "Mister." But I was intrigued and sometimes astonished by the first names I would see on my class roster.

Knowing that I would have to pronounce some of these names at graduation time, I often had to ask the graduate for the correct way to pronounce his first name.

So, because my class roster often bore no resemblance to that of a USD roster, I collected names over the years and would like to record them in this memoir.

Diana Spinney

Aasen, Arif, Aureliano, Ango, Ascion, Ashanti, Braulio, Condelario, Crispin, Chastis, Christoble, Cleararthur, Chai, Darness, Dashonn, Dante, Dagoberto, Dayjon, Delshon, Delfino, Deandre, Donanciano, Edy, Edin, Efrain, Eloy, Ervey, Ermulo, Eliodore, Eladio, Easerio, Estaban, Excell, Fausto, Faustini, Fedensio, Frazeil, Giovani, Geronimo, Guillermo, Hoang, Israel, Ismael, Isaha, Jhai, Jerrod, Jakovie, Jererai, Justo, Livante, Marin, Maximino, Mustafa, Norlando, Osbalde, Pao, Pearb, Phog, Quatrel, Quincy, Rigoberto, Rocendo, Rondrea, Romero, Sahr, Shon, Salvador, Sergio, Starsky, Tarone, Tariq, Tou, Trinity, Tywone, Utorn, Wiley, Viggo, Vernoil.

This could make up a great Spelling and Pronunciation Test!

I also think of my classes when I read this quotation from Jimmy Carter:

> We become not a melting pot
> but a beautiful mosaic.
> Different people, different beliefs,
> different yearnings, different hopes,
> dreams.

29

Graduations

You measure the size of the accomplishment by the obstacles you had to overcome to reach your goals.

Booker T. Washington

One of the things I was most grateful for to CCA was their attitude concerning a formal graduation for inmates who have earned their GED.

We had caps and gowns, tassels were ordered for each class, pictures were taken, family could be invited, programs were printed, music was provided, and refreshments would be served.

From my diary on June 27:

Graduation again and all went well until we found out that

a family had been sent away because they were too early. I was told that I need to tell more people in the prison that it is graduation day. I will be certain to tell the front desk and Master Control. Everyone from our department helps so much; couldn't do it by myself. Hope I let them know how much they are appreciated.

The program, front page, announced the class and date. Inside left side of the program listed the date, the processional, invocation, warden's welcome, guest speaker, and speeches from the valedictorian and salutatorian (based on GED test scores), presentation of diplomas, and benediction.

The program right inside listed the graduates and, as often occurred, some had been transferred out of the facility after completing all requirements but weren't around to participate in the formal ceremony. I needed to have 15 GED completions before I could schedule a graduation.

Sometimes this happened rather quickly and sometimes it took several months.

The program I am looking at as I write was the second graduating class of the year 2013. It listed 22 graduated, and 1 transferred out.

The backpage listed the administration, academic and vocational instructors and, always, the quotation at the top of this chapter.

I was responsible for finding a speaker for each graduation. I think I had used every pastor in Burlington and half of the pastors in Goodland before I retired. One graduation the speaker didn't show, so I was the fill in. Another graduation I remember because the pastor from Goodland came with his wife. But she was too frightened to come into the visitation room for the ceremony and stayed out in the waiting room. (I think she is part of the reason for writing this memoir because I think too many people have a misconception about prisons.) I can't think of a safer place to be these days!

The processional indicates that we had music, and we brought that up many stages over all the graduations that I was in charge of.

We started with "Pomp and Circumstance" on the piano. Thank goodness for my years of piano lessons! Then another teacher took over and we had an inmate who was really proficient. By the May 2013 graduation, we had progressed to the prison Jazz Band! (And that brings forth a 4 star memory for sure.)

A family was attending this graduation from Grand Junction and a young girl (4 or 5?) in a beautiful pink dress was dancing at the reception as the Jazz Band played. It was the prettiest scene I ever saw in that visitation room.

I bought film and each graduate had his picture taken before we marched in and we also had a group shot.

Refreshments were served and for the first few graduations, I had to fill out the necessary forms to have a cake or cookies prepared in the prison kitchen. I think it was our third graduation and the kitchen forgot! What they rushed to fix and brought to the visitation room was practically inedible! So, from then on, I did the cakes, usually four. (Thank goodness for cake and frosting mixes.) Later on, we even added ice cream and punch or pop and, with the help of my fellow teachers, we got it all done.

From my diary May 29, 2003:

It's Bob Hope's 100th birthday and the CCA vice-president came to visit. No connection there! But he visited with me and asked about number of graduations and graduates we had since we opened(1999). I had all the figures - but not totaled. (They are now totaled!) We have just passed the 200 mark in number of graduates.
He–very insightfully–said, "That must make you feel good" and he's right; it does.

I guess I realized at this time that KCCC, being a private prison, had to respond to its officers with numbers that show that the Education Department is doing its job. It wasn't the reason I had taken this position, but I guess the numbers showed me that I was accomplishing my goal of helping these inmates obtain their GED.

> So numbers:
> 1999-2001 = 108 GEDs
> 2002(New test) - 213 = 825 GEDs
> Total: 933 GEDs and 43 Graduations

When I look back at all the graduations I was a part of and remember all the smiling faces of families–and a few crying mothers–and the fellow inmates who could attend and celebrate with their friends, I think of one of my favorite quotes; this one from Ralph Waldo Emerson:

> "Scatter Joy"

And you can't do it by yourself!

P.S. A while back in this memoir, I mentioned that I had received only two phone calls from mothers. The mother who had made me promise never to let her son quit despite having failed the GED Math test 6 times, and who hired an inmate to work with her son, had also promised that she would be in attendance when he graduated. Well, she didn't make it because she couldn't leave her job in California at that time, but she sent a telegram thanking all of us who aided him in achieving his GED. Thanks are always appreciated.

P.P.S. Do you know how difficult it is to bring an iron into a prison? This question came to mind when I remembered all the graduations I was responsible for. The robes had to be stored in boxes after each graduation and put away somewhere for safe keeping. This meant that before each graduation, I had to have these gowns issued to me and they were always very wrinkled. I would bring my iron from home and practically sign my life away to bring it into the prison and, then, I got to iron them! (I guess this is a bit of prison trivia I dredged up!)

30

Classes I Taught for MCC

Those who bring sunshine into the lives of others cannot keep it from themselves.

James M. Barrie

Because I had a Master's Degree, I was eligible to teach classes for Morgan Community College at the prison. There were some inmates who had their GED and could pay the tuition who wanted to take college classes, and I was glad that I could do so.

I believe that tuition and fees for a three credit course when I began was $300.00. Some had that much money in their prison account and others were aided by funds coming in from family.

My students were all inmates who had earned their GED at the prison so they knew who their teacher would be, but I also had to have at least five enrolling to hold a class.

I taught some literature and speech classes, and before long, one student had enough credits that he was taking correspondence classes from outside. Fort Lewis College even had a program to aid incarcerated individuals in obtaining a bachelor's degree.

From my diary May 8:

Last test for my college classes. I really do not believe I will teach again for Morgan. I love the challenge and the students. I think I'm doing a good job altho' I have no one to pattern myself after. But I do want the college program to continue.

May 10:

I think the decision is being made for me. Beginning Summer 2003, Morgan Community College says you must have 8 in a class for full pay. I don't want to say that's impossible, but it will b e quite a challenge.

May 30

Made my last trip to MCC and turned in my grades for SPE115. Received a beautiful card from my five speech students. I hate the idea of never teaching college classes again, but since MCC raised the minimum class size to 8, I don't think we can make it.

When I prepared the college course history, I discovered that, in the five classes I taught for MCC, I had enough enrollment for the new rule of 8 students only once.

There is so much satisfaction for me in teaching the inmate college student; I will really miss it. I need to add here that Morgan Community College just raised tuition per credit, so this was a double whammy to the program.

P.S. The one drawback that I had not mentioned earlier is that I lived in Goodland, Kansas, so it was a 30 mile trip to work each day. Several of us teachers pooled our ride to work each day. When I taught college classes at the end of the school day, I had to drive myself to and from the prison on those days.

P.P.S. One of my students in a college writing class who had grown up in California wrote on seeing his father gunned down in his front yard when he was 8 years old. He had written so powerfully that I thought it should be submitted to Readers Digest or some place like that. So, you can see why I loved the college teaching. Many could write about things I never experienced, and I learned a lot!

31

Thank You

Thank you - a polite expression of one's gratitude

Webster's Universal Encyclopedia Dictionary

In my teaching days before I went to teach at the prison and even after retiring when I substituted in the schools in Goodland, I never heard a 'thank you' from a student.

Today, as I look through the gigantic folder I collected 'thank-yous' from my students and their families; I do have to fight back tears.

Some came on fancy cards, some in pencil on lined notebook paper, many on CCA/KCCC Inmate Request Forms. I wanted to include a few to show that these inmates are just human, too.

I like this quote from Jenji Kohan, the creator of the Netflix series Orange is the New Black:

> We all screw up, but we don't all get caught, which is why you can't paint everyone with the same brush. That's the basis of Orange is the New Black. Yes, the characters are criminals, but I prefer to define them by who they are rather than by what they've done. There's more to us than the moment we made a bad decision.

My students had to go to school because they had not graduated from high school, but they said, "Thank You" for the opportunity to take the GED (and prepare for it) on prison time. Their thank-yous were what gave me the feeling of success in my teaching in the prison.

I really feel that our kids today do not know what a gift education is to them. And because it is a gift, they need to thank a teacher.

John Ruskin:

> "In order that people may be happy in their work, these three things are needed. They must be fit for it, They must not do too much of it. And they must have a sense of success in it."

P.S. Since I was a teacher, not a Case Manager, I did not know the offenses for which my students were incarcerated I have to admit that with some of my students. I was a little curious, but I really did not want to know!

Dear Mrs. Spinney   1-10-04

    May God bless your heart! Thank you so very much for sending me my tassle. I know you did not halft to send it so <u>thank you</u>!
    I also wanted to thank you for helping me get my G.E.D. but as you know they moved me before graduation so thank you for that. I thought you were a wonderful teacher. I never thought I would ever say this but I enjoyed attending your class.
    I just wanted to drop you this quick note to let you know I thank you for everything from the bottom of my heart.

                    Thanks Again

                          Troy Lee Boldra

Diana Spinney

Hello Ms. Spinny   4/12/05

Hello, just wanted to tell you that I passed my G.E.D. with a 329, wow, I know what your thinking, you wish I could go to the graduation, me too, they don't have that here.

Ms. Spinny, I just want you to know that you have been the second most influential person to help shape me into a normal American, and thank you. The books that you had me read really taught me the whole perspective of the country I live in, and the great conversations we had, sublime!

On the subject of books, I started writing my first on 1/28/05, and have finished six chapters for a total twenty four thousand words at one fourth of the projected chapters. It is a book on End Time Prophecy and Revelation, and as a first book who knows if it will go to press, however as soon as I drop the pen on this one I will pick it back up and start my second book. Its so much fun writing, my life is arranged around my writing time. Its what I do, who I am, I write. And yes I still don't have a dictionary.

Ok life is good, I get out this year and will work as an electrician's aprentice untill the Lord puts me in fulltime writing or ministry. I have been drug free for over eleven years now so it's a win, win situation for me, and yes Ms Spinny I will send you any books that go to press!

                    Your Friend
                    John S. Chisholm
                        On the narrow path forever and,

Fourteen Years Behind the Wall: They Said Thank You

Diana Spinney

CORRECTIONS CORPORATION OF AMERICA
KIT CARSON CORRECTIONAL CENTER

INMATE REQUEST

TO: (Check One) ☐ Warden ☐ Classification ☐ Case Manager _____
☐ Asst. Warden ☐ Programs ☐ Unit Manager _____
☐ Security ☐ Medical/Dental ☒ Other MS SPINNY EDU

FROM: Inmate Name: James Johnson | D.O.C. Number: 127462 | Unit: SP401 | Job/Assignment: _____ | Date: 06 MAY 06

REQUEST: They just packed me out. Thank you for everything. I read 72 books in 3½ mo. of which The Moon Tattoo was the last. You opened my mind up to many, many new things. Without you I could not have done it.

Thank you for all of your support for my husband and our family at graduation.
Thank you
Brandy & Kids

MRS. SPINNEY,
I WAS VERY SORRY TO HEAR THAT YOU WILL NOT BE TEACHING ANY MORE COLLEGE CLASSES. I JUST WANTED TO THANK YOU FOR YOUR PATIENCE AND YOUR ACCESSIBLE TEACHING STYLE. YOU HELPED ME APPRECIATE POETRY! NO SMALL FEAT.
I PLAN TO PURSUE MY EDUCATION WHICH, WITHOUT YOUR INITIAL FOSTERING, I MAY NOT HAVE EVER CONSIDERED...
SO THANK YOU.
SINCERELY,
JAMES MCKINNEY

Thank you Mrs. Spinney
I owe my G.E.D. to you. You are very persistent in your classroom.

Edward DeLos Santos

Fourteen Years Behind the Wall: They Said Thank You

Diana Spinney

A typical graduation group, just before marching in

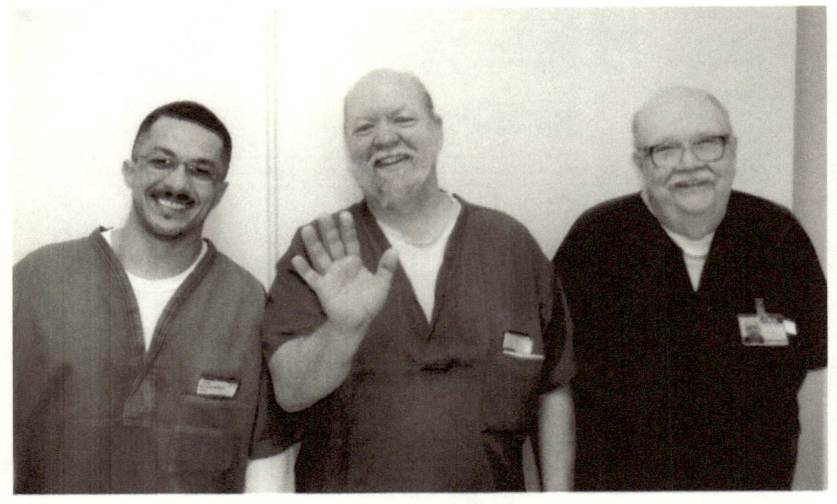

My great tutors

Fourteen Years Behind the Wall: They Said Thank You

Diana Spinney

> What you have done will be remembered in my heart!
>
> MS. Spinny Thank You
> good look'n out for me with the College stuff. its cool having a D.OC. mom (!!)
>
> THANKS
>
> Travis Hladik
> 10996
>
> May the Lord repay you for what you have done.
> RUTH 2:12 NIV

> Mrs. Spinney
> I want to say Thank You! for making this happen for me, it took awhile to get this, but you had the patience to tell me that I could do it and not to give up. You pushed me until you knew that I can do it. And thanks for the pictures they came out great and the graduation ceremony was so cool, I had a fun time and the goodies in the end a plus. You are a true Blessing keep up the good work.
>
> Your Student
> P. Martin

RESPONSE This goal I was personally committed to achieve, and I did.
Ms Spinny, one thank you is not enough, it's important to me to let you know how thankful I am for all your help. I sure am going to miss coming in the class room now.
Is it possible if I can come in from time to time and study?
Sincerely Thanks
Allen James

> thank you for all of your help with my GED. and keeping me on track and focused on my work and telling me I can do it
>
> thank you.
> D. Benavidez

> Each of your considerate and considerable actions towards those willing to learn, will be eternally remembered by both the students and their families.
> I conclude with an appropriate quote for you.
> "Blessed is the influence of one true soul on another."
> George Eliot

Fourteen Years Behind the Wall: They Said Thank You

> Ms. Spinny,
>
> I know that I thanked you personally on 10-8-04 when I found out that I finally received my GED, but to me that wasn't enough.
>
> You were apart of this achievement, you let me come in twice a day, and although at one time as you know I wanted to almost give up struggling in math, but I didn't. Through your encouragement and dedication, and care, and concern that you give as a person aswell as a professional you helped me along the way to be able to accomplish

A GIFT OF LIFE

A teacher is a warm loving person who will fully share their experiences of life, and the knowledge of the things that are in life. They are patient and determined to help in every way within their power. They set out to teach us how to understand. They are the key to the world's learning process,, the foundation of education and the seed of wisdom. Without the teacher there wouldn't be a world! But, because of the dedication to growth and prosperity of life that they have, they are like gardeners that are grooming their plants and flowers. They strive to enhance our intelligence bit by bit until we grow from knowledge into wisdom which flourishes into the preceptor of evolution.

Written by Michael A. Wilson
1-1-05

> Dear Ms. Spinney,
>
> Recently, I've gotten a disciplinary infraction, which has changed my current custody from medium security to closed custody and I'm awaiting a transfer to another prison.
>
> I wanted to leave you with a short message thanking you for making a difference in my life. Without your help and efficiency in proctoring my testing I wouldn't have accomplished or been able to accomplish my goals. Once again, Thank you so much!! May God bless you in all your endeavors!
>
> Sincerely,
> Richard Pearson
>
> P.S. Have a great day
>
> Date: 02-12-13

Diana Spinney

> Ms Spinney Thanks For every Thing I enjoyed having you as a teacher I hope and pray only good things For you Take care
>
> In Christ
>
> 3-21-05

SALUTATORIAN ADDRESS

Good morning everyone — on behalf of my fellow graduates we would like to thank you all for attending our graduation ceremony.

I am sure my classmates feel the same way that I do and would like to thank the education staff for all of their help, support, and guidance. I would like to give a special thanks to Ms. Rinehart and Ms. Spinney for all of their hard work, patience and encouragement they provided their students every day.

I hope all of us here today go on to do bigger and better things in our lives and take it upon ourselves to further our education and never get tired of learning.

Thank you,
K. Mudick

> October 5th
>
> Ms Spinney,
> I wanted to take a moment and thank you again for the time and energy you've given to my son Brian. I can't thank you enough for your efforts to show all those who want to earn their GED that it's worth it. I was very touched by your sincere thoughts the day of graduation.

32

Appreciation

Appreciation is a wonderful thing; it makes what is excellent in others belong to us as well.

Voltaire

I have to admit that from the beginning I felt a sense of appreciation from my students. I knew that many had dropped out of school, some many years ago, and now weren't sure about this have to go to school thing.

    I was pretty sure that if I could start them with something that they could do well in, we'd be on the way, and it seemed to work. (Practice tests would show me their strong and weak points.)

    I was certainly pleased with the many thank yous I received

Diana Spinney

from my students, but I was also happy when I received thanks from family, and I have tried to show you in some of their notes.

As I have told you, I had 7 principals in my 14 years at Kit Carson and consider the principal my boss, so I was very pleased to receive recognition and thanks from wardens and even a writeup in the Corrections Corporation of American newsletter. So, I have included copies of these in this chapter.

I believe everyone wants to be appreciated in their work and all of these 'thank-yous' went a long way in making me happy to teach in Burlington at the Kit Carson Correctional Center.

Fourteen Years Behind the Wall: They Said Thank You

Educator with an Attitude: Diana Spinney

"A GED is an essential thing in the marketplace. You need a GED to work at McDonalds."

So says Diana Spinney, GED instructor at Kit Carson Correctional Center (KCCC). Over the past seven years, she has educated approximately 400 inmates preparing to earn their GED. While she's held in high esteem by the facility principal, other teachers and inmates alike, Spinney never expected to find herself in education, much less teaching in a correctional setting.

"I didn't set out to be a teacher, I was going to be a dietician," she says. But with marriage on the horizon and an uncertain future ahead, she needed to have a job anywhere she and her family moved. Little did Spinney know her career would soon take another unexpected turn.

"At my class reunion, I told my best friend that I had applied to teach at a correctional facility, and was pretty sure I would work there," Spinney says. "She was shocked and tried to discourage me from working in a prison. She took me to another classmate to help talk me out of it, but he turned out to be a warden."

Thus began Spinney's journey as a corrections professional – a journey into uncharted territory. "I didn't know what to expect," she says, but she was soon met with numerous pleasant surprises.

"When I taught in the public schools; I really hated it," she says. "The students just didn't seem to care. And when I came to the prison, I found out they do."

Spinney began her career at KCCC teaching a class called Adult Basic Education 1 (ABE1), moved on to teach pre-GED classes, and has served as a GED instructor for nearly eight years. The GED tests five subject areas: reading, social studies, science and writing skills and Spinney's class helps inmates sharpen their reading, writing and math skills in preparation for the exam. Inmates must earn a certain score on the practice tests to be able to take GED. "Once they pass a test, then they're on their way," Spinney says.

And her impassioned approach to her work plays no small role in this process.
"She's very dedicated to what she does and she stays after it until it gets done, just like a bulldog. She gets a hold of the students and won't let them go. It means a lot to her to have them complete program," says Kay Gansemer, ABE1 instructor for students who speak English as a second language at the facility.

"She's a phenomenal teacher. She's certainly an asset here at the facility," says facility principal, Sherriccia Jackson.

"I look at myself as an encourager," Spinney says. "Many of our students don't have faith in themselves and I just feel that I'm there to direct them along the way and tell them that they can do it; It's a matter of attitude."

Her students are living examples of the dynamic impact she makes.

"Mrs. Spinney is an excellent teacher. She makes the learning process easy for us," says one of her students. "I originally felt nervous going into the process of earning my GED," says another student. "But Mrs. Spinney's encouragement helped to boost my confidence, and now I feel like my goals are so much more attainable." Although Spinney has been highly acclaimed by many other students who earned their GED under her instruction, she maintains a humble disposition. "They thank me but I didn't do it; they did. It is very rewarding to me," she says.

Now a seasoned educator, Spinney doesn't see an end to her career anywhere in sight. "I'm going to hang in as long as I can navigate the halls," she says, without hesitation. And for the duration of her time in education, she'll undoubtedly continue to impress upon the minds of her inmates the same lesson she's taught them for years: "Once you have your GED, no one can ever take that away from you."

© 2008 Corrections Corporation of America. All Rights Reserved.

Diana Spinney

CCA

Kit Carson Correctional Center
Educational Programs
This is to certify that

Ms. Spinney

She is accepting this award of:
Most Inspiration Teacher of The Year
This 29th day of October 2007

Principal   Date 10/29/07

Fourteen Years Behind the Wall: They Said Thank You

Diana Spinney

LETTER OF RECOGNITION
FOR
DIANA SPINNEY
KIT CARSON CORRECTIONAL CENTER
DEPARTMENT OF EDUCATION

This letter is being written to recognize Mrs. Diana Spinney for her nine years of dedicated, loyal, and professional service to CCA, KCCC, the Department of Education, and... more importantly, for all of the students whom she has served and helped achieve their GED.

Mrs. Spinney helped open the doors of Kit Carson Correctional Center at its first conception in 1998. During these nine years of service Mrs. Spinney has seen a minimum of one thousand (1,000) student inmates go through her classroom, with at least five hundred (500) of them attaining their GED. What a great job of making such a large difference in the lives of so many inmates. Thank you for caring!

In addition to her work in the classroom, Mrs. Spinney has always been willing to be a team player in regard to helping other staff members in the Department of Education and throughout the KCCC Facility. We especially enjoy all of the home cooked meals she has cooked and graciously shared with us. Again, thank you for all that you do for our KCCC inmates and staff.

Don Howell, Principal   Warden Hoyt Brill

Fourteen Years Behind the Wall: They Said Thank You

Diana Spinney

FROM THE BEGINNING 1998
TO THE ENDING 2013

February 13, 2013

To: Principal Jasnau:

Fourteen years ago, I applied for a position as Academic Instructor at a new prison opening in Burlington, Colorado. My family, my friends, even acquaintances were against this: their cries of "You can't work in a prison!" still resound in my head.

I did get that position at Kit Carson Correctional Center and began work there in October 1998. It has been my privilege to work with hundreds of inmates during this time and be responsible for helping over 800 inmates earn their GEDs.

It is with some regret that I must tender my resignation from KCCC effective February 28, 2013. At age 72, the body starts to fail, possibly the mind also!

But I must conclude with this - of all the various positions I have chosen in my working career, I saved the best for the last.

The following statements were not part of my resignation letter but I have included them in this memoir for your information.

My starting salary in 1998 was $28,000.
My ending salary in 2011 was $40,515.50

I am not sure I would have retired at this time, but my husband and I had a three-week trip to Alaska planned. I knew there would be no substitute teachers for my class and did not want my students to miss three weeks of study toward pursuing their GED goal.

Acknowledgements

The more important an activity is to your soul's evolution, the more resistance you will feel for it.

Stephen Pressfield

For many years, my husband and friends have urged me to write something. After all, I majored in English in college, but I am a lazy writer, and all I ever wrote was the annual Christmas letter.

But then came 14 years of teaching in a prison and I really wanted to let people know that ideas they had about prisons and inmates were not correct.

I believe that purchasing Oprah Winfrey's latest book *The Path Made Clear*,* a collection of thoughts from many famous people, was meant to happen as I found this quote from Oprah,

Diana Spinney

herself:

What I know for sure is that no matter how much wealth you come to possess, everything passes and changes with time. What is real, what is forever, is who you are and what you are meant to share with the world. That is your true treasure.

And then, many thanks to Susan Lessiak, the mother of my most favorite student in all my years at the prison. She came to visit all the way from Massachusetts and never ceased in thanking me, even after her son was transferred to another prison and I resigned from teaching at KCCC.
She also never stopped sending yearly reminders in the years since to "share my memories of the prison years."

So it is finished.

And I say "Thank you."

August 2019

*The Path Made Clear - Discovering your Life's Direction and Purpose. Oprah Winfrey, Produced by Melcher Media, 2019

www.ingramcontent.com/pod-product-compliance
Lightning Source LLC
Chambersburg PA
CBHW021956290426
44108CB00012B/1100